Watching an evening primrose bloom rekindles one's sense of wonder.

Carol Bishop Hipps
20th-century American writer

9 8 7
Digit on the right indicates the number of this printing

ISBN 1–56138–364–3

Cover design by Toby Schmidt.
Front cover illustration: *Anemones and Arnunculus* by Eileen Goodman.
Collection of Mr. and Mrs. Norman Saye, Pennsylvania.
Back cover illustration: *Asters* by Eileen Goodman.
Courtesy Locks Gallery, Philadelphia.
Interior design by Nancy Loggins.
Interior illustration by Khai Tran.
Edited by Melissa Stein.
Typography: ITC Berkeley by Deborah Lugar.
Printed in the United States.

This book may be ordered by mail from the publisher.
Please add $2.50 for postage and handling.
But try your bookstore first!

Running Press Book Publishers
125 South Twenty-second Street
Philadelphia, Pennsylvania 19103–4399

Flower

N O T E B O O K

An Illustrated Journal
with Space for Notes

RUNNING PRESS
Philadelphia • London

Deep in their roots, all flowers keep the light.

Theodore Roethke (1908–1963)
American poet

. . . Rain-awakened flowers,
All that ever was
Joyous, and clear and fresh. . . .

Percy Bysshe Shelley (1792–1822)
English poet

if the flowers bloom indiscriminately, we can accept such favors.

Marvin Bell, b. 1937
American poet

Sometimes I considered the whole bed of tulips, according to the notion of the greatest mathematician and philosopher that ever lived, as a multitude of optic instruments, designed for separating light into all those various colors of which it is composed.

Joseph Addison (1672–1719)
English writer and statesman

The poppy is painted glass; it never glows so brightly as when the sun shines through it . . . always it is a flame, and warms the wind like a blown ruby.

John Ruskin (1819–1900)
English writer and critic

I like my geraniums to fight, to clash in eternal contests of color, to wage their petalled arguments in perpetual debate, and in order that they do so there must be every sort of red, scarlet against magenta, cherry versus brick, crimson anti puce. . . .

Beverley Nichols (1898–1983)
English writer

. . . the unexpected discovery of a wild hyacinth, with its three slender bells of artless blue swaying in the wind, has all the charm of a stolen joy.

Colette (1873–1954)
French writer

The dandelion's pallid tube
Astonishes the grass,—
And winter instantly becomes
An infinite alas.

Emily Dickinson (1830–1886)
American poet

You've seen lilacs wet by rain? Perfect—a mingling of diamond bracelets and Concord grapes.

Allan Gurganus, b. 1947
American writer

In the dooryard fronting an old farm-house near the white-wash'd palings,
Stands the lilac-bush, tall-growing with heart-shaped leaves of rich green,
With many a pointed blossom rising delicate, with the perfume strong I love,
With every leaf a miracle. . . .

Walt Whitman (1819–1892)
American poet

. . . the garden flourishes and is quite glorious again, for the great blue spires of delphinium are in flower, also white Madonna lilies, and here and there a Japanese iris, luminous pale blue or violet.

May Sarton (1912–1995)
Belgian-American writer

. . . how these grand rambling Roses . . . rush up and tumble out, and make lovely dainty wreaths and heavy-swagging garlands of their own wild will.

Gertrude Jekyll (1843–1932)
English writer

In the old days, you had to be careful when you gave someone a posy of flowers. If they knew the language of flowers, they might think you were trying to give them a secret message. Red chrysanthemums meant "I love," and four-leaf clover meant "Be mine." But hydrangeas meant "Heartless" and Michaelmas daisies meant "Goodbye."

Elizabeth Laird, b. 1943
American writer

*N*o two men see the same iris.

A. S. Byatt, b. 1936
English writer

. . . the rose is not a means of communication like any other. It is already a message in itself.

Alain Meilland
20th-century American rose breeder

What a pity flowers can utter no sound! A singing rose, a whispering violet, a murmuring honeysuckle—oh, what a rare and exquisite miracle would these be!

Henry Ward Beecher (1813–1887)
American clergyman and editor

Roses grow upon briars, which is to signify that all temporal sweets are mixed with bitter. The briary, prickly bush grows before that; the end and crown of all is the beautiful and fragrant rose.

Jonathan Edwards (1703–1758)
American writer

*W*here you tend a rose . . . a thistle cannot grow.

Frances Hodgson Burnett (1859–1924)
English-born American writer

Some flowers spoke with strong and powerful voices, which proclaimed in accents trumpet-tongued, "I am beautiful, and I rule." Others murmured in tones scarcely audible, but exquisitely soft and sweet, "I am little, and I am beloved."

George Sand [Amandine A. L. Dupin] (1804–1876)
French writer

My face in the flower thou mayst see.

Edith M. Thomas
19th-century American poet

The true rose, the miracle of nature, owed nothing to the hand of man.

Iris Murdoch, b. 1919
Irish writer

I perhaps owe having become a painter to flowers.

Claude Monet (1840–1926)
French painter

The entire wall was covered with roses. They were a living fire, a mantle of burning, golden-hearted pure pink. The entire wall seemed to shimmer with life and light and health. The very air around it seemed suffused with radiance. You could . . . see that wall of roses for fifty miles. . . .

Anne Rivers Siddons, b. 1936
American writer

*B*ut who can view the ripened rose, nor seek
To wear it?

George Gordon, Lord Byron (1788–1824)
English poet

When I cut flowers, I never leave one alone on the bush, always leave behind a friend—or cut them all so they can come into the house together.

Joan Rivers, b. 1933
American entertainer

I can enjoy flowers quite happily without translating them into Latin. I can even pick them with success and pleasure. What, frankly, I can't do is arrange them.

Cornelia Otis Skinner (1901–1979)
American writer

. . . cut flowers last longer in the vase if one gives them a kiss every morning.

Romain Gary (1914–1980)
French writer

. . . the flowers . . . sweet-lipped as children. All night they've been breathing in the hall, dropping their pollens, daffodils, pink and red tulips, the hot purple and red-eyed anemones.

Sylvia Plath (1932–1963)
American poet and writer

Arranging a bowl of flowers in the morning can give a sense of quiet in a crowded day—like writing a poem, or saying a prayer.

Anne Morrow Lindbergh, b. 1906
American writer

. . . flower scents . . . only recall pleasant memories.

. . . I enjoy flowers as much when they get old and dried out as when they were fresh. I don't know—I just look at those flowers, and in my mind, I still see the beauty they once had. I never throw any of them away.

Van Cliburn, b. 1934
American pianist

I picked one of the tiny chandeliers of the honeysuckle and held it to my face.
The long stamens tickled, and the scent was thick and maddeningly sweet,
like a dream of summer nights.

Mary Stewart, b. 1916
English writer

The odor of heliotrope, more than any other plant, can surround me with memories of other days, other times; can stir my imagination to scenes of dainty ladies receiving courtly gentlemen to afternoon tea, of an opera party in the 'nineties with the guests in full regalia assembling in the box overlooking the stage. There is something intoxicating about the odor and as I bury my nose again and again in the fragrant cluster, more memories, more scenes crowd around me.

Rosetta E. Clarkson
20th-century American writer

Through the open door
A drowsy smell of flowers—gray heliotrope
And white sweet clover, and shy mignonette
Comes faintly in, and silent chorus leads
To the pervading symphony of Peace.

John Greenleaf Whittier (1807–1892)
American poet

There were no dark trees here, no tangled undergrowth, but on either side of the narrow path stood azaleas and rhododendrons . . . of salmon, white, and gold, things of beauty and of grace, drooping their lovely, delicate heads in the soft summer rain.

Daphne du Maurier (1907–1989)
English writer

. . . roses. . . . always smell like pepper and ginger.

Rosemary Simpson, b. 1942
American writer

I know a little garden close,
Set thick with lily and red rose,
Where I would wander if I might
From dewy morn to dewy night.

William Morris (1834–1896)
English artist and poet

I desired the owner of the garden to let me know which were the finest of the flowers; for that I was so unskillful in the art, that I thought the most beautiful were the most valuable, and that those which had the gayest colors were the most beautiful.

Joseph Addison (1672–1719)
English writer and statesman

I dote on my seedlings as though they were children. I am there to feed them, groom them, and point them in the direction of the sun. At their height of color, that delicate point of balance between youth and maturity, I gather them to my table, and savor them in all their delicious glory.

Anna Viadero
20th-century American writer

How easy it is to overlook the furry yellow comb inside the throat of an iris. . . .

Diane Ackerman, b. 1948
American writer and poet

For three days I have been watching its largest bud, a tiny golden pod. Tomorrow, the forsythia will be sprinkled all over with golden stars.

Karel Čapek (1890–1938)
Czech journalist and writer

Gardens have always been places of enchantment. Whether large or small, simple or elaborate in design, elegant or ordinary, it is there that the heart of man may rest from its cares and where life may renew itself.

Josephine Craven Chandler
20th-century American writer

How fair is a garden amid the toils and passions of existence.

Benjamin Disraeli (1804–1881)
English statesman and writer

Where flowers degenerate, man cannot live.

Napoleon I (1769–1821)
Emperor of France

*F*lowers and sunlight, air and silence—*"luxe, calme et volupte."*

Patricia Simon, b. 1934
American writer

Y*ou can live a long time with a geranium.*

Winston Churchill (1874–1965)
Prime Minister of England

A house with daffodils in it is a house lit up, whether or no the sun be shining outside. Daffodils in a green bowl—and let it snow if it will.

A. A. Milne (1882–1956)
English writer and poet

*A*t my garden-room window four incredible pink roses pressed against the glass as if trying to see in. Four rogue roses blooming and peering. The last roses of summer in January, trying to give me heart.

Susan Trott, b. 1937
American writer

Thy smiles I note, sweet early Flower,
That peeping from thy rustic bower
The festive news to earth dost bring,
A fragrant messenger of Spring.

Samuel Taylor Coleridge (1772–1834)
English poet and critic

*H*ow precious are the flowers of mid-winter! Not the hothouse things. . . .
the genuine toughs that for some strange reason elect to display themselves
out-of-doors at this time of the year.

Vita Sackville-West (1892–1962)
English writer

. . . it so happened that a Christmas cactus had chosen this moment to bloom. Its lush blossoms, fuchsia-shaped but pure red rather than magenta, hung at the drooping ends of strange, thick stems and outlined themselves . . . against the glistening background of the frosty pane—jungle flower against frostflower. . . .

Joseph Wood Krutch (1893–1970)
American writer and educator

You cannot forget if you would those golden kisses all over the cheeks of the meadow, queerly called dandelions.

Henry Ward Beecher (1813–1887)
American clergyman and editor

. . . there are few dramas more rewarding than the sequence of wildflowers that through the spring and summer spring from the ground. . . . in the most unlikely places.

Howard Ensign Evans, b. 1919
American entomologist

*E*ven the majestic cañon cliffs, seemingly absolutely flawless for thousands of feet and necessarily doomed to eternal sterility, are cheered with happy flowers on invisible niches and ledges wherever the slightest grip for a root can be found; as if Nature, like an enthusiastic gardener, could not resist the temptation to plant flowers everywhere.

John Muir (1838–1914)
Scottish-born American naturalist

*S*pring *teased and flirted with the mountains, then finally opened herself in a rich flurry of wildflowers and birdsong.*

Daranna Gidel, b. 1948
American writer

Wildflowers are survivors. Like many of us, they are "immigrants" who crossed America in covered wagons or on horses' hooves, many with legends of their own.

Claudia Alta ("Lady Bird") Johnson, b. 1912
First Lady of the United States

. . . there are places on this earth clear all the way up
and all the way down
and in between a various blossoming
the many seed shapes of the many things
finding their way into flower or not,
that the wind scatters.

Robert Hass, b. 1941
American poet

I remember vividly . . . one special field, absolutely crammed with golden buttercups. . . . A great field full of golden buttercups on early summer is something indeed.

Agatha Christie (1890–1976)
English writer

In the springtime, one could travel for hundreds of miles on a bed of flowers. Sometimes they came up to my stirrups.

Anonymous 19th-century Texas Ranger

Yellow japanned buttercups and star-disked dandelions—just as we see them lying in the grass, like sparks that have leaped from the kindling sun of summer.

Oliver Wendell Holmes (1809–1894)
American writer and poet

And, as it works, the industrious bee,
Computes its time as well as we.
How could such sweet and wholesome hours
Be reckoned, but with herbs and flowers.

Andrew Marvell (1621–1678)
English poet

M*ornings, I drank dewdrops on magnolia flowers;*
Evenings, I ate the fallen petals of autumn chrysanthemums.

Ch'u Yuan (343?–289 B.C.)
Chinese poet

The buttercup catches the sun in its chalice. . . .

James Russell Lowell (1819–1891)
American poet

*E*verywhere the lanes were fragrant with Wild Roses, and Honeysuckle, and the breeze came to us over the hedges laden with the perfume of the clover-fields and grass-meadows. . . .

Edith Holden (1871–1920)
English naturalist

Blossom by blossom the spring begins.

Algernon Swinburne (1837–1909)
English poet

*B*rave flowers—that I could gallant it like you,
And be as little vain!

Henry King (1592–1669)
English poet

How beautiful are the retired flowers! how would they lose their beauty were they to throng into the highway crying out, "admire me I am a violet! dote upon me I am a primrose!"

John Keats (1795–1821)
English poet

Big doesn't necessarily mean better.
Sunflowers aren't better than violets.

Edna Ferber (1887–1968)
American writer

The daisy is a perfect little democracy . . . it's the highest of flowers. . . .

D. H. Lawrence (1885–1930)
English writer

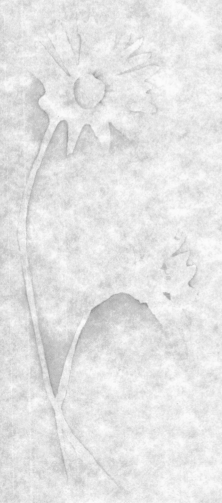

Daffodils, that come before the swallow dares,
And take the winds of March with beauty.

William Shakespeare (1564–1616)
English dramatist and poet

I never saw daffodils so beautiful. . . . they verily laughed with the wind that blew upon them over the lake.

Dorothy Wordsworth (1771–1855)
English diarist

The roaring moon of daffodil and crocus. . . .

Alfred, Lord Tennyson (1809–1892)
English poet

Across acres of old pastures, where the goldenrod are taking over, late August and early September turn the land into a tumbling sea of the richest yellow. The fields are awash with waves of goldenrod that flow across the slopes and break against the stone walls and the woods.

Edwin Way Teale (1899–1980)
American naturalist and writer

I lie amid the Goldenrod,
I love to see it lean and nod. . . .

Mary Clemmer (1839–1884)
American poet

Peonies have an intoxicating smell, and they're so soft and creamy looking. I like the pale pink ones best, but there's a whiteish-yellow one called Prairie Moon that's magical. Their foliage remains beautiful all summer.

Tasha Tudor, b. 1914
American writer

*E*ach rose that comes brings me greetings from the Rose of an eternal spring.

Rabindranath Tagore (1861–1941)
Hindu poet

[They] were engaged in setting out bowls of roses in a long row across the floor. Big bowls, packed tight with blossom. Thousands of petals, ripe-blown and silkily smooth, like the cheeks of innumerable little cherubs. . . .

Aldous Huxley (1894–1963)
English writer

They crowded around the flowers, touching the delicate petals. It was like dipping their fingers into rainbows, for there were irises of every color ranging from deep violet to swan white.

Nancy Thayer, b. 1943
American writer

The flowers of the field are the children of sun's affection and nature's love. . . .

Kahlil Gibran (1883-1931)
Lebanese philosopher and poet

. . . there is never a time when there is not a flower of some kind out, in this or that warm southern nook. The sun never sets, nor do the flowers ever die. There is life always. . . .

Richard Jefferies (1848–1887)
English writer

Art is the unceasing effort to compete with the beauty of flowers—and never succeeding.

Marc Chagall (1887–1985)
Russian painter

Infinite numbers, delicacies, smells,
With hues on hues expression cannot paint,
The breath of Nature, and her endless bloom.

James Thomson (1700–1748)
English poet

The thing that makes the flowers open and the snowflakes fall must contain a wisdom and a final secret as intricate and beautiful as the blooming camellia or the clouds gathering above, so white and pure in the blackness.

Anne Rice, b. 1941
American writer

. . . 'tis my faith that every flower
Enjoys the air it breathes.

William Wordsworth (1770–1850)
English poet

Who loves a garden still his Eden keeps,
Perennial pleasures plants, and wholesome harvests reaps.

Amos Bronson Alcott (1799–1888)
American educator and philosopher